_____

_____

_____

_____

PERLA COLLECTION

ISBN 978-1-911424-97-0
SKU/ID 9781911424970

Cover design by Fabio Perla
"LIKE A DREAM"
Monochrome pencil on wood - size cm 60 x 60 - Year 2013

Book design by Wolf
Editor: Wolf

Publishing Company:
Black Wolf Edition & Publishing Ltd.
2 Glebe Place, Burntisland KY3 0ES, Scotland
www.blackwolfedition.com

Copyright © 2016 by Black Wolf Edition & Publishing Ltd.
All rights reserved. - First Edition: 2016

Name _____

Surname _____

Address _____

_____

Phone _____

Mobile _____

E-mail _____

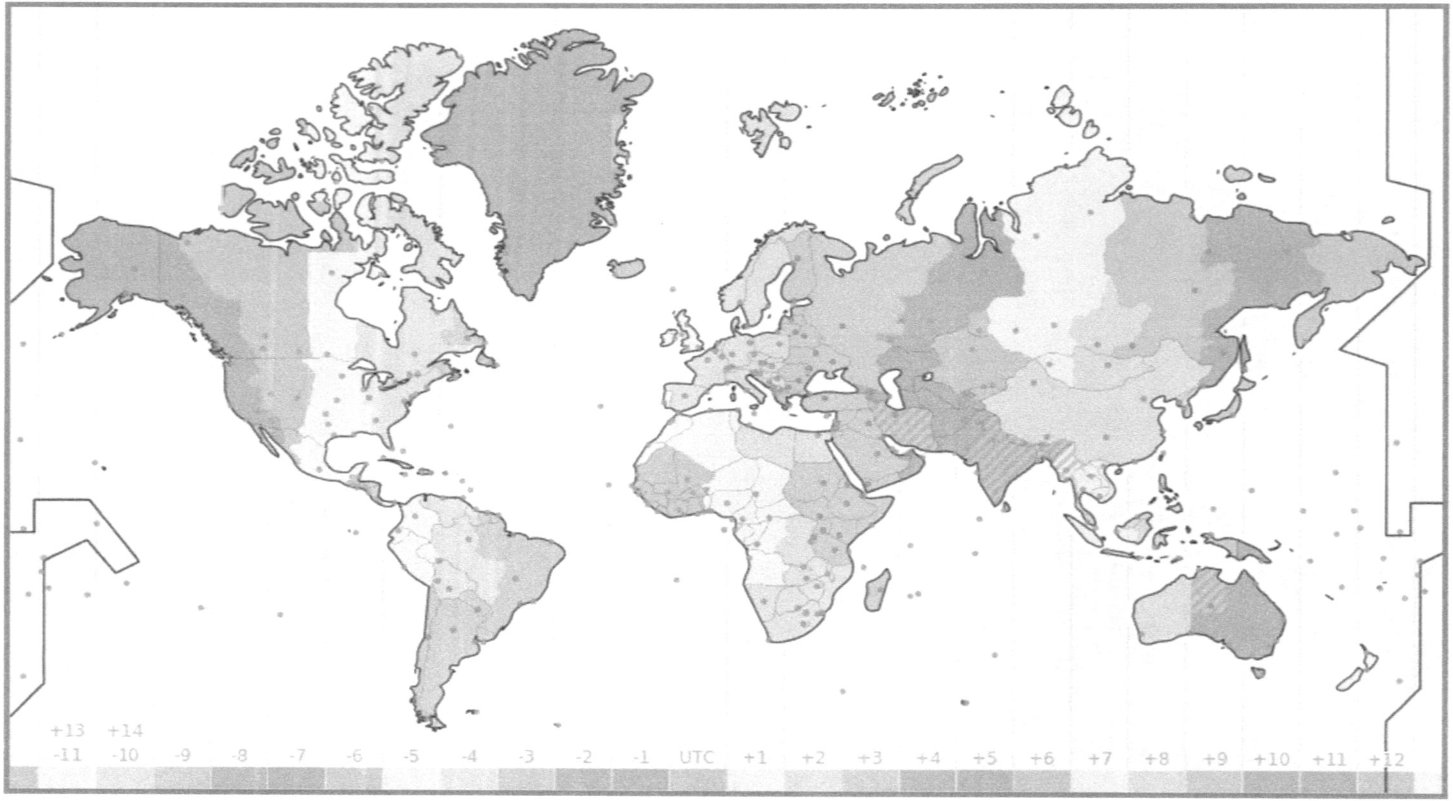
+13 +14
-11 -10 -9 -8 -7 -6 -5 -4 -3 -2 -1 UTC +1 +2 +3 +4 +5 +6 +7 +8 +9 +10 +11 +12

PERLA COLLECTION

SKETCHES

ISBN 978-1-911424-97-0
SKU/ID 9781911424970

Cover design by Fabio Perla
"LIKE A DREAM"
Monochrome pencil on wood - size cm 60 x 60 - Year 2013

Book design by Wolf Graham
Editor: Wolf Graham

Publishing Company:
Black Wolf Edition & Publishing Ltd.
Scotland
www.blackwolfedition.com

Copyright © 2016 by Black Wolf Edition & Publishing Ltd.
All rights reserved. - First Edition: 2016

www.ingramcontent.com/pod-product-compliance
Lightning Source LLC
Chambersburg PA
CBHW020107240426
43661CB00002B/70